St Columba by William Wilson

IONA

A GUIDE
TO THE
MONUMENTS

JOHN G DUNBAR
IAN FISHER

Revised by IAN FISHER

RCAHMS

Edinburgh: HMSO

Lobster-fishing on east coast

INTRODUCTION

Yellow iris in flower on
St Columba's day, 9 June

The small Hebridean island of Iona has an historical and religious importance out of all proportion to its size. The monastery founded in 563 by the Irish monk Colum Cille or Columba became a missionary centre and the head of a family of monasteries in Ireland, Scotland and northern England. The mission from Rome that landed in Kent in 597 (the year of Columba's death) had little success in Northumbria, and that kingdom was converted by Irish monks from Iona who came to Lindisfarne about 635. Although this mission to Northumbria lasted less than thirty years, Iona remained one of the greatest centres of the Irish church until the Viking attacks of about 800.

Irish Christianity was strongly ascetic in character, and many monastic founders preferred island sites for their communities. These usually consisted of a number of monks living in separate huts, grouped round a small church or oratory and normally enclosed by a ditch or rampart. Their lives, although often of great austerity, were less strictly regimented than those of the monastic orders of the Middle Ages, and their buildings, normally made of timber, were correspondingly modest. In fact the visitor today will see few standing remains of the great days when Iona was one of the centres of early Christianity, the existing abbey church being a medieval building which served a later Benedictine foundation.

Abbey and Dùn I
from Sound of Iona

7th-century grave-marker, inscribed on top edge *Lapis Echodi* ('the stone of Echoid')

The whole island, however, is a monument to Columba and his monks, for the life of the saint by abbot Adomnán, written in Latin about a century after his death, allows us to identify areas where he retired for prayer and meditation or his monks worked the fields. Local tradition records other places associated with Columba, and he was so closely identified with the island that for centuries its Gaelic name has been *I Chaluim Cille* ('I of Colum Cille'). The name *I* was derived from an ancient Celtic word for 'yew tree', and Adomnán used the Latin form *Ioua insula* ('the yewy island'). The

Shepherd at work

modern name originated with a medieval misreading of *Ioua*, which perhaps gained currency because the word *Iona* happened to be the Hebrew equivalent of the Latin *Columba* ('a dove').

Whether, as local legend asserts, Columba landed on Iona in 563 by chance while seeking a place from which his native Ireland was not visible, or as the result of careful preparation and negotiation, the island proved well-adapted to the needs of an Early Christian monastery. Grazing and fishing were freely available, crops could be grown on the light soils of the machair (a sandy plain close to the west shore), and the more sheltered eastern coast included an area of gently-sloping ground suitable for the erection of buildings. During Columba's time, and for several centuries thereafter, these were constructed mainly of wood, wattle and turf, although by the 7th century some structures were large enough to require the shipment of substantial timbers from the Scottish mainland. In the following century, however, stone was similarly imported to make large crosses, and for the major stone buildings of the Middle Ages local flagstone and granite boulders were supplemented by sandstone from Carsaig on the south coast of Mull.

Irish monks had a well-deserved reputation as bold sailors and travellers and the earliest records of the monastery contain numerous references to boats, some of them timber-built and others of skins stretched over wickerwork frames, in the manner of Irish currachs of the present day. Several beaches on the east coast provide landings for small boats, but there is no satisfactory harbour for larger vessels and without expert knowledge the main sea-approaches are hazardous. No doubt it was for this reason that many early visitors to the monastery chose to travel by way of Mull, shouting from the opposite shore for a ferry-boat to come from Iona.

During the century following the establishment of the

Cattle on east coast

The Virgin and Child with angels:

(right) Book of Kells

(far right) St Oran's Cross, detail of shaft

4

monastery of Iona, the Columban Church played a leading role in the expansion of Christianity in Britain, notably through the conversion of at least some of the Picts of eastern Scotland and the re-introduction of the faith to Anglo-Saxon Northumbria by St Aidan. This mission to Lindisfarne also had important results for scholarship and art, for the ensuing cross-fertilisation of Irish and Northumbrian culture produced a flowering of literature, manuscript illumination and sculpture, in which Iona was a major participant. Indeed, the celebrated Book of Kells, one of the masterpieces of Hiberno-Saxon art, was probably written and illuminated on Iona during the middle or second half of the 8th century, while the remarkable group of High Crosses was created at the same period. In these, traditional Irish skills in timber construction and metalwork design were combined with Northumbrian innovations in stone-carving to create one of the most enduring monuments of Early Christian art, the Irish ringed cross. This period of outstanding creativity was brought to an end by the onset of Viking raids shortly before 800. Soon afterwards most of the community were transferred to a more secure location at Kells, in eastern Ireland, and although religious life continued to attract monks and pilgrims to Iona, its influence was much diminished.

The foundation of the Benedictine abbey at the turn of the 12th and 13th centuries brought Iona into the mainstream of medieval monasticism. Its layout was modelled upon that of other Benedictine houses throughout western Europe and the monks followed the usual pattern of daily work and worship. But whereas the Columban monastery had extended its influence far beyond the West Highlands, the medieval abbey remained an establishment of local importance, whose lands lay entirely within Argyll and the Hebrides. Its abbots and benefactors were invariably drawn from local families, and its much-prized exemption from episcopal authority depended upon the support of its principal patrons, the MacDonald Lords of the Isles. When the Lordship was forfeited at the end of the 15th century, the abbey lost its independent status and passed into the possession of the bishops of the Isles, who began to lease its lands and revenues to powerful laymen. Following the Reformation of 1560, which ended almost a thousand years of monastic worship on Iona, Charles I in the 1630s established the abbey church as the cathedral of the Isles. Although some repairs were carried out, the Civil War brought a speedy end to this

Machair and west coast

15th-century effigy of Prior Cristin MacGillescoil

Repairing sacristy door in abbey

proposal, and subsequent local attempts to maintain the church for parish use were no more successful.

Fortunately, however, much of the abbey and the nearby nunnery survived, and their remains, with associated sculpture, today form the most conspicuous monuments on Iona. In these buildings, as in the earlier High Crosses, the craftsmen of Iona took varied influences and translated them into a recognisably local version of medieval European architecture. Not surprisingly, since the West Highlands shared the same society and culture as Gaelic-speaking Ireland, that country provided many of the models and, in the earlier period, probably the masons themselves. Even in the 13th century, however, motifs from lowland Britain such as dog-tooth ornament are found, treated in a repetitive but rich manner. During the 14th century little building took place, but a distinctive school of monumental carving developed on Iona so that a group of native craftsmen was available to carry out major late medieval schemes of reconstruction at the abbey and nunnery. Their work, although sometimes lacking technical expertise, shows a vigour and ornamental inventiveness which give it a special place in Scottish medieval art.

Although no effective steps to preserve the ruins of Iona were taken until the Victorian period, early travellers to the West Highlands were quick to emphasise their importance. Two detailed first-hand descriptions of the island's antiquities were compiled before the end of the 17th century. As facilities for travel improved in the following century, and particularly after the 'discovery' of Staffa in 1772, there was a steady increase in the number of tourists, many of whom recorded their experiences in print or graphic form. Distinguished visitors whose writings inspired others to make the arduous journey included Bishop Pococke, Thomas Pennant and Dr Samuel Johnson with James Boswell. They were followed after 1800 by Sir Walter Scott, John Keats, Felix Mendelssohn (who travelled on

Abbey from east, c. 1761

Abbey from west, c. 1872

Abbey from north-east, 1772

6

an early steamboat-excursion) and William Wordsworth, who wrote four sonnets to commemorate the occasion.

During the Victorian period scholars such as William Reeves and William Skene began to take an active interest in the history and architecture of Iona, and their investigations drew attention to the poor condition of many of the buildings and tombstones and prompted efforts to preserve them. Following earlier repairs, a major programme of consolidation was carried out at the abbey and nunnery in 1874-6 by the Edinburgh architect Rowand Anderson, for the proprietor, the 8th Duke of Argyll. In 1899 the Duke made over the ownership of the principal buildings, including the abbey, the nunnery and St Oran's Chapel, to a body of Trustees known as the Iona Cathedral Trust. Under the terms of this gift the Trustees were bound to re-roof the abbey church and restore it for worship, and they completed this in 1910. The building was subsequently used by the island's Church of Scotland congregation until the renovation of the parish church in 1939. In 1938 the late George MacLeod (Lord MacLeod of Fuinary) founded the Iona Community as a Church of Scotland brotherhood, centred on Iona but dedicated to a life of Christian witness and mission throughout Scotland and beyond, and this opened the way for the restoration of the monastic buildings. Work began in the following year to designs by the architect Ian G

Lindsay, and operations were completed in 1965. In 1979 the island of Iona (with the exception of the buildings transferred to the Iona Cathedral Trustees in 1899) was sold by the Trustees of the 10th Duke of Argyll to the Fraser Foundation, who presented it to the Scottish nation in memory of the late Lord Fraser of Allander, and ownership was transferred by the Secretary of State for Scotland to the National Trust for Scotland. At the same time the Iona Cathedral Trustees launched an appeal and established a team of craftsmen to repair the principal buildings and to preserve the island's historic and architectural heritage for future generations.

Sculptor carving capital in cloister

Boat at pier

ISLAND TOUR

– 1 –
THE VILLAGE

This area of the island has for long been the main centre of population, as well as the principal landing point for visitors and goods. Roads linking the landing-places at St Ronan's Bay and Martyrs' Bay to the nunnery and abbey were constructed during the Middle Ages, and the early farmhouses were scattered round them. The present village street overlooking St Ronan's Bay was laid out soon after 1800, when the farms and crofts were reorganised. Many of the granite-built houses date from the second half of the 19th century and replaced earlier thatched cottages. Just beyond the north end of this street stands Bishop's House, a retreat-house founded in 1894 by the Scottish Episcopal bishop of Argyll and the Isles; the design is by the Inverness architect Alexander Ross.

(Above left) Bishop's House

(above) Houses in village street

(left) Village street and abbey from pier

Iona Psalter,
David playing harp

– 2 –
THE NUNNERY

This house of Augustinian canonesses, dedicated to St Mary the Virgin, appears to have been founded about 1200 by Reginald son of Somerled, ruler of the Isles. The first prioress was Reginald's sister, Beatrice (Bethoc), who may have been the first owner of the fine 'Iona Psalter', now in the National Library of Scotland. The nucleus of trained nuns required for the foundation was probably brought from Ireland, where houses of the Augustinian Order were numerous. Like most other Scottish nunneries, that on Iona has little recorded history, but the community was evidently small in number, with modest landholdings mainly on the island of Mull, including the island of Inchkenneth, and the south end of Iona itself. The last two prioresses were members of the MacLean family and at the Reformation the revenues came into the hands of the MacLeans of Duart, from whom they passed in about 1690 to the Campbell Earls of Argyll.

Although far from complete, the group of buildings is one of the best-preserved examples in the British Isles of a typical small medieval nunnery. The church itself was built during the first quarter of the 13th century, but the cloister and south range of conventual buildings were rebuilt during a period of late medieval reconstruction, which may have marked a revival in the fortunes of the community. The ruins were described by most 17th- and 18th-century visitors to Iona, the principal object of attention being the graveslab of Prioress Anna MacLean (d.1543), then preserved in the chancel. The earliest drawings show that by the 1760s little more survived than at present, except for the east wall and vault of the chancel which collapsed about 1830, damaging Prioress Anna's monument. In 1874 the 8th Duke of Argyll initiated a programme of site-clearance and repair, and in 1899 he transferred the buildings to the Iona Cathedral Trust. Plans for a full restoration were prepared in 1917 by the architect P MacGregor Chalmers; in the event, however, work was confined to the repair of the north chapel and the laying out of the cloister garden.

The church comprises a single-bay chancel, a nave and north aisle of three bays, and a north chapel, with a small room above the vault, at the east end of the aisle. The nave, formerly separated from the stone-paved chancel by a timber screen, was no doubt occupied largely by the nuns' stalls, but there may also have been provision for the laity either there or in the adjacent aisle, which had its own chapel and altar. During the late medieval alterations a gallery was built at the west end of the nave, and at the same time the

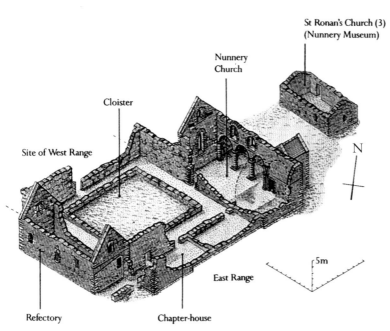

Cloister

Site of West Range

Nunnery Church

St Ronan's Church (3)
(Nunnery Museum)

N

Refectory

Chapter-house

East Range

5m

arcade was walled in to form a second chapel in the north aisle.

The mason-work of the church is of good quality, and both the chancel and the north chapel have been rib-vaulted - a rare occurrence in medieval West Highland architecture. Certain elements of the design are best paralleled in Ireland and it is probable that some at least of the work-force were of Irish origin. Among the most conspicuous of these features are the boldly-framed windows in the west wall of the nave and east wall of the north chapel (the latter one triangular-headed), and the external corner-shafts of the chancel. The placing of the high-level clearstorey windows above pillars rather than arches allowed a reduction in the height of the wall-head, and made for greater stability in the rubble masonry. Like the decorative stepping of continuous string-courses, well seen in the chancel, this structural device was particularly favoured in Ireland. All of this work is Romanesque in character, as are the sculptured capitals of the arcade, but the collapsed chancel

arch was acutely pointed and the dog-tooth ornament in the north chapel resembles the earliest Gothic work in the abbey. The corbels inserted to support the nave-gallery of about 1500 also contain some interesting carvings, including a representation of the Annunciation.

The conventual buildings were grouped round a cloister-garth on the south side of the church. Of the cloister itself only the wall-footings remain, but fragments are preserved in St Ronan's Church. These show that the late 15th-century arcade was of elaborate design, comprising cusped ogival arches on paired circular shafts and springing from rectangular corner piers, all richly moulded and carved in the characteristic local style.

The east range of buildings comprised three main rooms at ground-level, the upper storey no doubt being occupied by the nuns' dormitory. The central room was the chapter-house, which preserves stone benches around the walls, while the compartment next to the church may have housed a parlour, together with a timber stair giving access to the dormitory above.

Nothing now survives of the west range, which extended under the modern road, but the south range stands entire on three sides. This was originally a single lofty chamber serving as the nuns' refectory, but in the 16th century its eastern part was floored at an intermediate level and adapted for domestic occupation. Above one of the windows facing the road to the south there is a much-weathered *sheela-na-gig*, a female exhibitionist figure of a type found more frequently in Ireland than Scotland.

Graveslab of Prioress Anna MacLean, 1543. The missing portion showed the Virgin and Child

North chapel

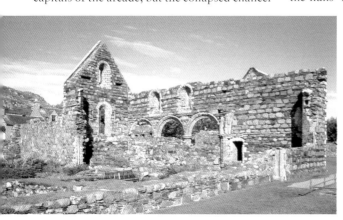

Church from south-east

MacLean's Cross, west
face of cross-head

– 3 –
ST RONAN'S CHURCH
Nunnery Museum

During the Middle Ages, and perhaps for some years after the Reformation, this building served as the parish church of the island. It dates from the late 12th or early 13th century and, like most West Highland churches of that period, is a small single-chambered structure with no architectural embellishment. The triangular-headed south window repeats a feature of the north chapel of the adjacent nunnery. In 1923 the church was restored as a museum for carved stones, from the nunnery and elsewhere, and it was reorganised for the same purpose in 1993.

Excavation in 1992 showed that the church was built on the site of a very small Early Christian chapel, whose clay-mortared south and east walls were incorporated into the foundations of the medieval building. This chapel in turn was built above earlier graves, and when the church was abandoned some time after the Reformation it was again used as a burial-place. The excavated remains confirmed the statements of Dr Samuel Johnson and other visitors that until about 1760 the nunnery area was reserved for female burials.

Excavation in St Ronan's
Church, 1992

– 4 –
MACLEAN'S CROSS

This cross stands in its original socket-slab, close to the former junction of the three medieval streets that linked the main landing-places to the nunnery and abbey. Both faces bear interlaced foliage typical of the Iona school of carving, and in the west face of the cross-head there is a representation of the Crucified Saviour, clothed in a long robe of archaic form. At the foot of the east face there is an armed horseman, presumably a MacLean chief who commissioned the cross in the second half of the 15th century.

MacLean's Cross and parish church

— 5 —
THE PARISH CHURCH and MANSE

For nearly two centuries until 1828 Iona lacked any resident minister or place of worship, but in that year a parliamentary church (so called from an 1824 Act which provided funds for new churches and manses in the Highlands) was built to a standard design, under the supervision of Thomas Telford. In the original arrangement of the interior, as shown in early photographs displayed in the church, the pulpit stood against the centre of the east wall and a long communion-table was aligned along the main axis. The adjacent manse was of Telford's single-storeyed type, but its central block was heightened early in the 20th century. It now houses the Iona Heritage Centre, with displays on the geology and social history of the island.

Cairn, Blàr Buidhe, from south-west

— 6 —
CAIRN, BLÀR BUIDHE

This grass-covered mound lying 60m west of the St Columba Hotel is one of the few prehistoric sites to have been identified on Iona. It measures almost 7m across, with a kerb of massive boulders, and is probably a burial-cairn of the second millennium BC. Island tradition in the 19th century identified it as a house belonging to the mythical Irish hero, Finn.

St Oran's Chapel, doorway

— 7 —
ST ORAN'S CHAPEL and REILIG ODHRÁIN

The chapel and burial-ground take their dedication from Oran (Odhrán), supposedly a cousin of St Columba. A medieval tradition recording his sacrifice and burial by Columba, to consecrate the island, has no historical basis.

The chapel is the earliest surviving standing building on Iona, and was probably erected as a family burial chapel by Somerled, 'king' of the Isles (d. 1164), or his son Reginald. Its rectangular plan, with a single doorway in the west wall, is characteristically Irish, while the chevron and beak-head ornament of the doorway also resemble Irish work of the third

St Oran's Chapel from west

quarter of the 12th century. The MacDonald Lords of the Isles continued to use the chapel as a burial-place during the later Middle Ages and the elaborate tomb-recess in the south wall may have been erected by John, 4th and last Lord of the Isles, who was forfeited in 1493. The building was restored and re-roofed in 1957.

The burial-ground, Reilig Odhráin, dates from the Early Christian period, but its relationship to the Columban monastery is uncertain. It is possible that it originated as a burial-ground for the secular aristocracy and that the early monastic cemetery lay near the west end of the abbey church. Early accounts drew attention to the numerous medieval effigies

Interior of St Oran's Chapel

and slabs commemorating members of leading West Highland families, 'the best men of all the Isles'. The most notable of these monuments, together with numerous Early Christian carvings discovered here, are now preserved in the Abbey and Nunnery Museums and the abbey cloister. Nothing is visible, however, of the tombs of the Kings of Scotland, Ireland and Norway who were reputedly buried here, and it is likely that many of these supposed burials are mythical. Beyond the north wall of Reilig Odhráin

can be seen a branch of the medieval paved street leading to the abbey. To the east of this is a modern extension of the burial-ground, where John Smith, the Labour Party leader, was buried in 1994.

Tomb-recess in St Oran's Chapel

Clay mould for glass stud

– 8 –
TÒRR AN ABA

This narrow spine of rock has been identified as the site of a cell used by St Columba which, as his biographer tells us, was 'built in a higher place' than the rest of the monastery and enjoyed a view of Mull. When the summit was excavated in 1957 the stone footings of a small squarish building were discovered, partly overlain by a medieval cross-base. Along the walls, which are now marked by a modern setting of mortared stones, were found stubs of charcoal, thought to represent stakes supporting the roof structure.

This may also be the 'little hill overlooking the monastery' from which Columba gave his final blessing. To the east there stood three High Crosses (pp. 16-17), and beyond them the medieval abbey church probably stands in the position of an Early Christian church. The remains of rectangular and circular timber buildings have been excavated south of Tòrr an Aba and in the triangle of ground between the medieval street and the large field. Immediately north of Reilig Odhráin the excavation in 1979 of a large ditch revealed shoes and other leatherwork, and remains of lathe-turned wooden bowls, from nearby workshops. Clay moulds and other evidence of high-quality metal- and glass-working have been found in the same area and also north-east of Tòrr an Aba. The excavated ditch, which probably dates from the early 7th century, was bounded by a hedge of hawthorn and holly, and it formed part of the complex of boundary earthworks known as the *vallum*, of which impressive standing remains can be seen to the west and north-west (p. 28).

Wooden bowls:
(above) replicas at Colmcille Heritage Centre, Garton, Co. Donegal

(below) original fragments

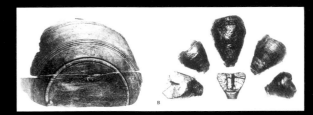

Excavation of ditch, 1979

Leather shoe and reconstruction

Glass rod and bead

– 9 –
THE HIGH CROSSES

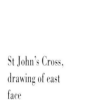

The free-standing crosses of Iona are among the outstanding examples of a type of monument which became popular in northern Britain and Ireland during the 8th century. In rural areas such crosses served as preaching-stations, while in monasteries they marked areas of special significance, such as entrances or burial-grounds, and provided focuses for public processions or private meditation.

Of the four most complete crosses of this type that survive on Iona, St John's Cross, St Martin's Cross and St Matthew's Cross were grouped west of the abbey, close to the presumed site of the early monastic church. The fragments of St Oran's Cross were first recorded in the 19th century in Reilig Odhráin, where there is a massive empty socket-stone. St Martin's Cross remains intact in its original granite base, but the others are now displayed in the Abbey Museum. St Matthew's Cross probably dates from the late 9th or early 10th century, but the other three from the middle or second half of the 8th century. Only in the case of St Martin's Cross, however, can it be shown that the present names were applied to them before the 19th century.

Although local craftsmen were no doubt experienced in the structural problems of timber crosses, and in the design of manuscripts and metalwork to which the ornament of the High Crosses was closely related, they may have been carved by stone-carvers brought from outside the Irish area, perhaps from Pictland. Some of the materials, too, were imported. The local schist used for St Oran's Cross evidently proved unsuitable, and the largest components of St John's Cross, as well as the slightly later St Martin's Cross, were carved from stone brought from the Mid Argyll mainland.

St John's Cross was returned to Iona for museum display in 1990, after extensive repair, and a concrete replica stands in the original base. Its arms have the widest span (2.2m) of any known cross in Britain or Ireland. Like St Oran's Cross, it was composed of several large pieces fitted together with mortice-and-tenon

St John's Cross, drawing of east face

St Martin's Cross, west face

16

joints, and it is likely that the ring was introduced during repairs after an early fall, thus inventing the 'Celtic' ringed cross. Both faces are divided into panels carved mainly with serpent-and-boss and spiral ornament; the circular recess at the centre of the west face of the cross-head formerly housed a large metal boss. The east face of St Martin's Cross is likewise decorated with serpent-and-boss ornament, while the west face bears figure-scenes, including the Virgin and Child, Daniel in the Lions' Den and Abraham's sacrifice of Isaac. The slots in the ends of the cross-arms probably housed applied metalwork decoration. Little but the broken shaft of St Matthew's Cross survives; the east face bears a carving of the Temptation of Adam and Eve, very similar to one on a cross at Kells.

St Matthew's Cross before removal to abbey museum

Abbey and crosses from Tòrr an Aba

St Martin's Cross, east face

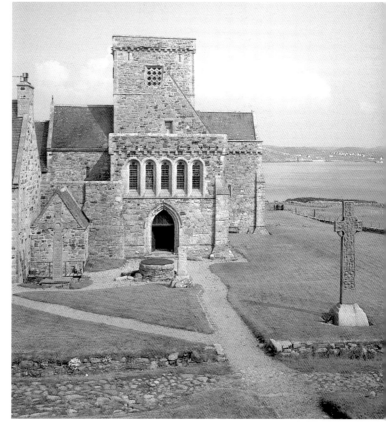

– 10 –
THE ABBEY

South window of choir

Abbey church from south

The abbey was founded about 1200 for Benedictine monks, despite the opposition of Irish churchmen who tried to maintain the older Celtic community. The reputed founder, as at the nunnery, was Reginald son of Somerled, but clearly all three main branches of Somerled's descendants approved the foundation. Its original endowments included lands throughout the regions that they controlled, in the islands of Canna, Coll, Mull, Colonsay and Islay as well as in the mainland district of Lorn. Reginald's descendants, the MacDonald Lords of the Isles, remained the principal patrons of the abbey until the end of the 15th century.

The abbey, which was dedicated to Saint Columba, stands near the centre of the area occupied by the early monastery and it is probable that the Benedictine church occupies the site of successive churches of the Early Christian period. The steady development of the buildings throughout the 13th century suggests that its early history was prosperous. The first church, built about 1200-20, comprised a square chancel, transepts with small eastern chapels, and a nave having aisles at the east end only; there was no provision for a cloister in its present position to the north. The plan is an unusual one, but the occurrence of certain Irish mannerisms, such as the continuous string-course, suggests that Irish masons were employed, although the chapels in

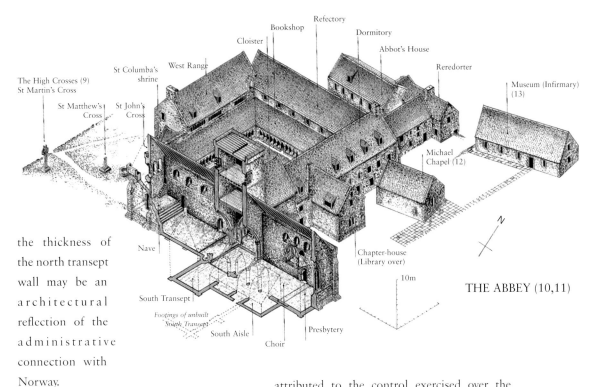

The High Crosses (9)
St Martin's Cross

St Matthew's Cross

St John's Cross

St Columba's shrine

West Range

Cloister

Bookshop

Refectory

Dormitory

Abbot's House

Reredorter

Museum (Infirmary) (13)

Michael Chapel (12)

Nave

Chapter-house (Library over)

South Transept

Footings of unbuilt South Transept

South Aisle

Choir

Presbytery

10m

THE ABBEY (10,11)

the thickness of the north transept wall may be an architectural reflection of the administrative connection with Norway.

During the second phase of building, commencing about 1220, the eastern arm of the church was considerably enlarged above an undercroft and the construction of the cloister and monastic buildings was begun. The extensive use of dog-tooth ornament during this phase suggests that masons from eastern Scotland were present although Irish features also occur, and the same combination of styles can be seen in the contemporary architecture of the nunnery. In about 1270 a most ambitious extension was begun, entailing the erection of a huge south transept probably intended to accommodate pilgrims viewing the relics belonging to the abbey. The only work completed was the lowest courses of the walls, now visible south of the choir and under grilles in the south aisle, although the abbey refectory seems to have been built at this period.

There is no evidence of further building until the middle of the 15th century, following a period of almost a hundred years of decline and internal dissension. These misfortunes were attributed to the control exercised over the abbey's affairs by the MacKinnon family; among the allegations made against the notorious Fingon MacKinnon, the 'Green Abbot (c.1357-1408), a kinsman of the chief of the clan, were moral delinquency, misuse of revenues and neglect of the monastery buildings. In 1421 it was claimed that the timber-work and masonry of the choir and bell-tower were collapsing.

After spending much of his career retrieving the abbey's fortunes, Abbot Dominic (1421-c.1465) was able, in about 1450, to begin a major reconstruction which continued almost to the end of the century. The two-level choir was replaced by a lofty and wider choir having a south aisle linked to an enlarged south transept. The nave was also rebuilt and widened to the south, and at the same time a substantial tower was erected over the crossing. This work was probably directed by Donald Ó Brolcháin, a craftsman of Irish descent whose signature appears above the ornate capitals of the south-east crossing-pier (p. 20-1, 2, 3).

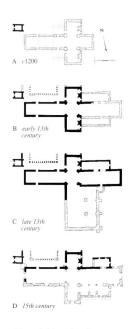

A c1200

B early 13th century

C late 13th century

D 15th century

Plans of abbey church showing new work of each period in outline

Carved capitals:
(right) south choir-arcade
(below) south-east pier of crossing

St Columba's Shrine

This is the name now given to the tiny steep-roofed building that stands a little north of the west doorway of the abbey church, and separated from St John's Cross by a small enclosure containing early graveslabs. Only its footings survived before it was restored as a chapel in 1962. It was formerly free-standing, and its plan and position suggest that it may have been an oratory of Early Christian date, comparable in size and proportions with the very smallest Irish stone churches.

St Columba's Shrine and west front of church

The buttress-like projections or *antae* at the ends of the west wall, which would originally have extended to roof-level, are a feature of these buildings. Two burial-cists preserved beneath the timber floor are probably medieval, but the local tradition, first recorded in the 1690s, that this was the original site of St Columba's tomb, is perfectly credible.

The Nave

This was the only part of the medieval church to require extensive rebuilding, which was completed to the design of P MacGregor Chalmers in 1910. The upper parts of the south and west walls belong to this period, including the distinctive five-light west window. The lower parts, including the west doorway and the small north-west angle-tower, are mainly of 15th-century date. The angle-tower has a multi-cusped window overlooking the nave doorway; the small chamber inside, entered by steps from the nave, preserves medieval plaster showing the impressions of the plank centering used to build its shallow vault.

Inside the west doorway, the squared sandstone masonry of the west wall of the narrower early 13th-century nave is still visible. It ends in an irregular scar south of the porch, where the original south wall was demolished in the 15th century, but part of this wall is preserved under a grille south of the font, and its continuation is marked in the paving of the lower central area of the nave. The change in levels, which is an unusual feature of the nave, appears to be an innovation of the 15th century. The north wall had been almost entirely demolished before the modern rebuilding, but the lowest stones in both doorways remain in position. Traces of three transverse walls have

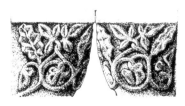

Carved head on west
arch of crossing

transept was gifted by Queen Elizabeth II in 1956, and the south chapel window contains a stained-glass representation of St Columba designed by William Wilson, RSA, in 1965.

The crossing dates mainly from the 15th century, but the high north arch of the earlier crossing remains visible above its successor. Some of the mouldings of the crossing-piers and arches are distinctly old fashioned, perhaps reflecting a lack of experience among the 15th-century masons, and there are signs that work was brought to a hasty conclusion. The massive two-storeyed tower is reached by a spiral stair at the south-west corner of the crossing. The upper storey, lit by elaborate traceried windows, contains the belfry above which there was formerly a pigeon-loft. The clock on the south belfry window replaces a medieval one in the same position, and there is one large bell cast at Loughborough in 1931.

East wall of north
transept

Within the 15th-century south transept there stand two marble monuments by Sir George Frampton, commemorating the 8th Duke of Argyll (d.1900) and his third wife, Ina McNeill,

Tower from south-west

been recorded in the nave, and one or more of these may represent part of an Early Christian church.

The Transepts, Crossing and Tower

The north transept is the only substantial part of the original Benedictine church of about 1200-20 to survive. Its style is late Romanesque, with small wide-splayed windows and plain round-headed arches having nook-shafts with moulded bases and capitals. One of the weathered capitals preserves foliage-ornament, and the capitals of the crossing were scalloped. A shaft in the north-east angle shows that it was originally intended to vault the transept, but its walls were heightened when the choir was extended about 1220. Between the two eastern chapels there is a niche for a statue, perhaps of St Columba, of which only the feet now survive. Against the west wall rises the reconstructed night-stair, which gave access from the adjacent monks' dormitory for night services. The oak screen at the entrance to the

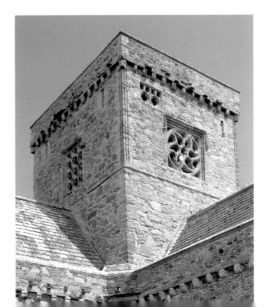

21

Sedilia and abbot's effigy in choir

Sacristy doorway

(Right) North wall of choir

who was buried there in 1925. A copy of the deed by which the Duke established the Iona Cathedral Trust in 1899 hangs on the west wall near the bronze screen, which bears his arms and motto. Cut into the east wall there is a well-preserved circular consecration cross. Immediately outside the south transept can be seen the footings of the large unfinished transept of the late 13th century, which was evidently intended to incorporate an eastern aisle of three vaulted bays. The plan of this remarkable structure was apparently modelled on that of the transepts of St Andrews Cathedral

The Choir

Like the transepts and crossing, the choir was restored to the designs of Thomas Ross and John Honeyman in 1902-5. The greater part of the building, however, belongs to the second half of the 15th century, while on the north side there are some remains of the original choir of about 1200-20 and of its two-level successor of about 1220-50.

These early fragments give clear indications of how the choir came to assume its present form. The most conspicuous feature of the north wall is the large double arch, ornamented with dog-tooth and supported on a circular column whose base stands about 1.8m above the present floor-level. This marks the level of

the enlarged choir of about 1220-50, and until the 15th-century rebuilding the arches gave access from the choir to a north aisle. Beneath the choir there was an undercroft having a timber roof supported on a mural ledge, parts of which can be seen below the west arch and further east below the north choir window. A blocked undercroft window is preserved in the latter area, and fragments of doors into its aisles are visible below the central pillar and under a grille on the line of the demolished south wall. The lower parts of the clearstorey windows and the stepped string-course, which linked the east arch with the original north window, also belong to the 13th century. The elaborate doorway beneath the east arch was inserted during the 15th-century reconstruction, when the arches were blocked and the aisle was converted into a sacristy.

The remains of the original Benedictine chancel of about 1200 are less obvious, being

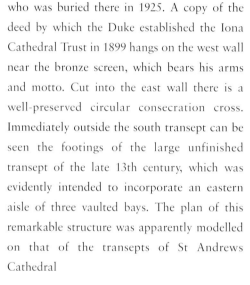

South-east pier of crossing

Capital in south choir-aisle, angel in West Highland armour

confined to the lower part of the north wall between the crossing and the double arch, whose masonry is composed mainly of local flagstone. A moulded sandstone string-course, interrupted by a possible blocked window, extends for about 5m along the wall-face and terminates abruptly at a point where the masonry shows signs of patching. This scar marks the east end of the original church of about 1200, which was demolished soon afterwards to allow the enlargement of the choir.

On the south side of the choir as rebuilt in the 15th century an arcade of three pointed arches opens into the south choir-aisle. The clearstorey windows are set above the pillars, as in earlier work at the abbey and nunnery, and at least one of the windows may be an early one in re-use. This aisle shows certain peculiarities of design and construction, including a last-minute reduction in width (evidenced by a line of projecting bonding-stones in the adjacent transept wall) and the use of clumsy internal arches to buttress the choir-arcade.

The most notable feature of the aisle is the fine series of carvings on the capitals of the arcade and adjacent crossing-arches. These carvings are closely related to the monumental sculpture of the Iona school, but show a variety of styles ranging from Romanesque to 15th-century social realism. The diverse subject-matter includes Biblical scenes such as the Temptation and Expulsion of Adam and Eve, the Virgin and Child between angels, and the Crucifixion, as well as mythical animals and foliaceous ornament. Depictions of contemporary life include an armed rider and foot-soldier, and a cow-killing scene which is treated in genre style with interesting details of secular costume. The south pier of the east crossing-arch bears an inscription which evidently named the principal carver, who was perhaps also the master-mason, of the 15th-century reconstruction; this is now damaged, but originally read: DONALDUS O BROLCHAN FECIT HOC OPUS ('Donald Ò Brolchán made this work').

The east end of the choir is lit by three large windows of flamboyant style, more similar to Irish than Scottish work of the period. This area was the presbytery, reserved for the clergy celebrating the daily monastic high mass. Close to the south window there are a piscina (a basin for pouring away the water used for washing the altar-vessels) and three sedilia (seats for officiating clergy) carved with foliage-ornament in West Highland style. The modern communion-table of Iona marble is set in a pavement of medieval sandstone slabs and occupies the site of the medieval high altar, whose slab was destroyed by souvenir-hunters during the 18th century; this likewise appears to have derived from the local marble-quarry (p. 29). On the second of the three steps leading up to the communion-table are set the

(Left) Effigy of Abbot John MacKinnon

(above) Capital in south choir-arcade, rider and foot-soldier

23

East end of choir

effigy attributed to Abbot Dominic (1421-*c*.1465) and that of Abbot John MacKinnon (1467-*c*.1498); both are portrayed in eucharistic vestments and the MacKinnon effigy incorporates a base-slab carried on four lions and bearing an elegantly incised inscription. On the same step, beneath the 19th-century Persian 'judgement carpet', there is the Tournai marble slab that held a late 14th-century Flemish brass, probably commemorating a member of the MacLean family.

The communion-table, along with the choir-stalls and the sandstone font with its Celtic ornament, were designed by P MacGregor Chalmers *c*.1912. The stained glass of the clearstorey windows was designed by Douglas Strachan in 1939 and shows Saints Columba, Brigid and Patrick and, on the south, Saint Margaret of Scotland. The embroidered cushions and kneelers for the stalls were executed by the Scottish Handcraft Circle to the designs of Adam Robson in 1963-9.

– 11 –
THE CLOISTER and MONASTIC BUILDINGS

In monastic houses throughout Western Europe, the buildings in which the monks lived and worked were grouped around a court or cloister. Its covered alley-ways linked the church to a communal dormitory on the upper floor of an east range which also included the chapter-house, and to a large refectory set parallel to the church. The decision to place the monastic buildings at Iona to the north of the church, rather than on the more usual south side, was no doubt dictated by the position of the stream, for running water was required to flush the reredorter or latrine block.

As first erected in the first half of the 13th century, the cloister-arcades had coupled octagonal columns with moulded bases and capitals decorated mainly with scalloped and water-leaf ornament. Numerous fragments are preserved, and some were re-used during the restoration of 1958-9. At each corner there was a group of four columns, but these were replaced in the 15th century by solid piers

Capital of south-east crossing-pier

(right) Abbey from north-west

linked by diagonal arches to the adjacent angles of the court, an arrangement which was maintained during the restoration. Many of the capitals of the new columns have been carved with individual designs of foliaceous and bird-ornament, and a large bronze by the Lithuanian sculptor, Jacques Lipchitz, representing the Descent of the Spirit, has been installed at the centre of the garth.

On the ground floor the east range contains the slype (a passage leading from the cloister to the detached buildings to the east), the chapter-house and two rooms, one of which was possibly used as a classroom for novice monks. The narrow compartment adjoining the north transept, originally the slype, was converted during the later Middle Ages into a private room. The chapter-house was rebuilt at the same period, but retains its original division into vestibule and inner chamber, separated by a handsome double arch similar in style to the contemporary north choir-arcade of the church. The monks met here daily to hear a chapter from the Rule of St Benedict and to discuss the business affairs of the abbey.

The dormitory on the upper floor of the east range is approached by a day-stair at the north-east corner of the cloister, as well as by the night-stair from the north transept. During the late medieval period it was probably divided into cubicles by timber partitions, and the present arrangement of bedrooms dates from the restoration of 1953. The room over the chapter-house is traditionally identified as the monastic library and was restored as such in 1938 in memory of Alexander and Euphemia Ritchie, former curators of the abbey buildings.

The north end of the dormitory is joined by a narrow link-building to the reredorter. Both structures were restored in 1942-3 to include storage and residential accommodation, but

the channel at the base of the reredorter, through which water formerly flowed to flush the latrines above, is still clearly visible. The building immediately to the west of the reredorter, which was restored in 1956 and is identified as the abbot's house, had its own latrine served by the same water-course.

The late 13th-century north range is occupied by the refectory, built above an undercroft which now contains the abbey bookshop. Its original north wall survives to full height and is supported by three massive buttresses with bevelled angles. Although now entered from the dormitory day-stair, the

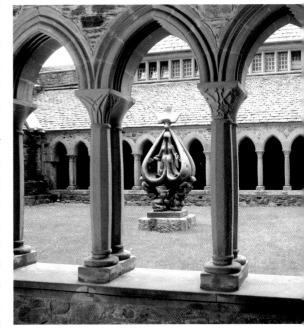

Cloister and statue by Lipchitz

refectory was originally approached through an elaborate doorway at the north-west corner of the cloister; its moulded arch is in-complete, and the stair to which it gave access has disappeared. The spacious interior of the refectory is lit by four original windows to the north and by a modern traceried window in the west gable. Within a projecting bay in the north wall is the pulpit from which, in accordance with monastic custom, readings were given during meals. The refectory was partially restored in 1875 but the main work of reconstruction was carried out to Ian G Lindsay's designs in 1949-50, and the existing screen and gallery, together with

14th-century effigy of
Gilbride MacKinnon

the massive tie-beam roof of Norwegian timber, date from that period.

The west range is the only one that does not stand upon medieval footings, and it seems that the substantial two-storeyed block completed to Lindsay's designs in 1965 is considerably larger than its predecessor. The north end of the medieval range probably incorporated the monastic kitchen. A little to the west, at the foot of Tòrr an Aba, may be seen the footings of an oblong building now laid out as a garden. Excavations in 1966-8 showed this to have been the medieval bakehouse and brewhouse.

Graveslab showing
cross and galley

– 12 –
THE MICHAEL CHAPEL

This is the southern of the two detached buildings that stand a little to the east of the east range. It is a typical chapel of West Highland type, with a narrow north doorway (widened during the restoration of 1959), and probably dates from the late 12th or 13th century. A 16th-century record of a burial-aisle dedicated to St Michael may well refer to this building. The restoration was largely financed by donations from Africa, and the stalls and the elliptical-curved ceiling are made of African timber.

– 13 –
THE ABBEY MUSEUM

A second detached building, standing north of the Michael Chapel, was probably the monastic infirmary. This would have provided residential care for aged and infirm monks as well as nursing facilities for the sick. Following extensive restoration in 1964, the building now serves as a museum and houses a selection of carved stones from Reilig Odhráin and elsewhere on the island. St John's Cross (pp. 16-17) was re-erected in the museum in 1990. The group of over one hundred Early Christian cross-marked stones on Iona is one of the richest in the British Isles, while there is an even larger collection of effigies, graveslabs and crosses of late medieval West Highland type. Many of these stones are displayed in St Ronan's Church, in the nave of the abbey church, and in the abbey cloister.

– 14 –
ST MARY'S CHAPEL

This chapel, in the field south of the abbey, probably dates from the 13th century. Only fragments of the side walls survive, but clearance in 1875 showed that it was about 18m long and had a north doorway. Its function in relation to the Benedictine abbey is uncertain, but the fact that a branch of the medieval street leading to the abbey ran past the chapel suggests that it was used by pilgrims as well as by the monastic community.

(left) Interior of
Michael Chapel

St Mary's Chapel from south-east

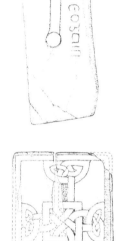

– 15 –
TIGH AN EASBUIG
The Bishop's House

This building, of which only the mid-wall remains standing, may have been erected by Bishop Neil Campbell in the 1630s, when the abbey church was briefly restored as the Cathedral of the Isles. According to a late-17th-century description, the larger division of the house contained a hall open to the roof and the smaller a buttery with a chamber above. Dr Johnson noted in 1773 that the ruin was one of only two buildings on the island to have a chimney.

– 16 –
CLADH AN DÌSIRT
The burial-ground of the hermitage

The only visible remains are those of a small rectangular building, probably a medieval chapel, lying within a walled or embanked enclosure. The two prominent gateposts flanking the original entrance to the enclosure were formerly spanned by a massive lintel.

The name suggests that these remains occupy the site of the *diseart* (from the Latin *desertum*, 'a desert') or hermitage whose superior was named, with other officials of the pre-Benedictine community on Iona, in a record of 1164.

Early Christian graveslabs

(Left) Tigh an Easbuig from south-west

Cladh an Dìsirt, drawing by Drummond, c. 1866, showing entrance-lintel

– 17 –
THE VALLUM

The *vallum* or rampart was a normal feature of an early Irish monastery and formed its symbolic and legal boundary. At Iona it took the form of a rectilinear earthwork enclosing an area of at least 8ha (20 acres), within which the principal buildings of the monastery (now super-seded by those of the Benedictine abbey) oc-cupied a more-or-less central position. Impressive remains of the earth-and-stone rampart with its ditch, and an outer bank in some places, are preserved at the north and west of the site. The alignments of other buried ditches, extending as far south as the St Columba Hotel, are known from aerial and geophysical survey and from excavation (p. 17).

Air view of vallum and abbey

– 18 –
LOCHAN MÓR
The great lochan
and
IOMAIRE TOCHAIR
Ridge of the causeway

This former loch, extending to the foot of Dùn I, was drained in about 1750 to provide the islanders with a supply of peat. The embankment of earth and stone (Iomaire Tochair) that bounds its south-west side may have been constructed as a road-way during the Early Christian period to give access from the monastery to the fertile west coast machair. The embankment probably served also as a mill-dam, for the stream that flows out of the lochan and passes north of the abbey is named Sruth a' Mhuilinn ('the mill stream').

– 19 –
COBHAN CÙILTEACH
The remote hollow

This name is now applied to the much-altered remains of a small circular hut, but probably was attached originally to the level area where it is situated, at the foot of Cnoc nam Bradhan. A tradition of antiquity attached to the site before the end of the 18th century, when the popular name 'Culdee's

Vallum and abbey from Dùn I

Cell' seems to have originated as a mistranslation of the Gaelic. While this may well have been the 'more remote place in the wilderness', overlooking the island of Tiree, to which St Columba withdrew for prayer, the date of the hut-circle is uncertain. The enclosure formed in the lee of a massive rock-outcrop about 30m north of the hut is probably a sheep- or cattle-pen of no great age.

include a gunpowder-store, a small rock-cut reservoir, a cutting-frame and a roughly built quay. The stone is white in colour, streaked with yellowish-green serpentine. It was used both for the medieval altar of Iona Abbey and for the present communion-table of about 1912 (pp. 23-4).

Dùn Cùl Bhuirg from north

– 20 –
DÙN CÙL BHUIRG

This small fort is the only monument of Iron Age date on the island and is comparable in size and situation to many of the prehistoric forts on Mull. Some remains of a defensive wall survive on the south and east sides of the summit. Excavations carried out in the interior in 1957-9 and 1968 revealed a small circular house, together with occupation debris which indicated that the fort was in use between the 1st century BC and the 3rd century AD.

– 21 –
THE MARBLE-QUARRY

It is probable that the marble veins of Iona were sporadically worked from a very early date, but the first documentary reference to quarrying occurs in 1693. The drystone house to the north ('the house of the lowlanders') was probably built when the quarry was being worked in the 1790s under the direction of R E Raspe (mineralogist and author of *Baron Munchausen*). The existing remains, from the most recent period of activity about 1907-14,

– 22 –
ST COLUMBA'S BAY

This small bay, also known as Port na Curaich ('harbour of the skin-covered boat'), is traditionally identified as the landing-place of the saint on his arrival from Ireland. The earliest travellers' accounts in the 1690s describe visiting the bay and collecting 'Iona pebbles' of serpentine from the shore. A grassy mound at the head of the shingle beach was reputed to perpetuate the size and shape of the saint's boat, but excavations in 1897 revealed no evidence of artificial origin. The cairns that stand on the raised beach of the adjacent bay to the west may have been constructed as a devotional act by medieval pilgrims.

Cutting-frame at marble quarry

St Columba's Bay from north-east

THE HISTORIC LANDSCAPE

Spring flowers

Although Iona measures only 5.5km in length, it displays a great variety of scenery – beaches of white shell-sand; grassy machair land and sand-dunes to west and north; the rocky summit of Dùn I, exactly 100m high; and areas of rolling heather moorland intersected by steep-sided grassy valleys. Most of the island is composed of pink and grey Lewisian gneiss, one of the most ancient of rocks, with a fringe of dark Torridonian flagstone along the east coast, and a few outcrops of marble, notably at the quarry (p. 29). The ice-ages brought a covering of gravel containing rounded boulders of red granite, and larger erratic granite blocks, which provided valuable building-material.

These varied natural resources have been exploited by man since the Mesolithic period (c.6500-3500 BC) and worked flints left by itinerant hunter-gatherers have been found in several parts of the island. Permanent farming settlement in the Neolithic period is reflected archaeologically by a decline in the pollen of scrub woodland and the appearance of plants typical of arable cultivation, while at least one stone axe of this period has been found on the island. Continuing occupation is indicated by the Bronze Age cairn (p. 13) and the Iron Age fort of Dùn Cùl Bhuirg (p. 29), but it is not certain whether Iona was still inhabited when Columba arrived in 563 AD.

The *Life of Columba*, written by abbot Adomnán about 700, gives vivid glimpses of

St Columba's Bay from west

(right) Martyrs' Bay from north

the island being used for arable and pastoral farming by the monastic community, and for prayer and meditation by Columba himself. He retreated for prayer to the 'little hill of the angels', the natural mound of Sithean ('the fairy hill') overlooking the Machair; to a 'remote place' which was perhaps Cobhan Cùilteach (pp. 28-9); and to the 'great fort',

Sunset on west coast

almost certainly Dùn I. The view from the summit embraces the Hebrides from Islay to Skye and west to Tiree, including islands where there were monasteries and hermitages dependent on Iona, as well as the distant mainland of Argyll. Later folk-tradition represented Columba as climbing Càrn Cùil ri Èirinn ('Cairn of [him who turned his] back on Ireland'), a summit in the south-west of the island, to verify that Ireland could not be seen, but the cairn there is modern.

Arable farming in Columban times was pursued mainly on the 'little western plain', whose Gaelic name, *An Machair* ('the small

plain') corresponds to the Latin name used by Adomán. This grassy area over-looks the 'Bay at the back of the Ocean' which provided abundant seaweed as fert- iliser for its light sandy soil, and it was cultivated until the 19th century. The *Life of Columba* also refers to dairy-farming and cattle, and the excavation of bones from the monastic area has confirmed their importance, as well as giving proof of fishing and seal-hunting.

Whether or not Iona was inhabited at the time of Columba's arrival, it is likely that a lay

population of craftsmen and farming tenants developed in succeeding centuries, as in many Irish monasteries. St Ronan's Church (p. 12) was built about 1200 for these laymen, who thereafter served as tenants of the Benedictine abbey or the nunnery. A massive turf-built boundary-wall, the black dyke of Staoineig, which crosses the island from coast to coast, was probably built in the medieval period to define the nunnery's property at the south end.

In the 17th and 18th centuries the island was farmed by a number of joint-tenants, paying rent to the MacLeans of Duart and, after about 1690, to the Campbells of Argyll. Their main crop was barley, grown on the western and northern machair, the central valley and the eastern plain, where the long ridges of plough- cultivation are still to be seen. They pastured cattle, their chief source of income, on the extensive common grazings, and some small oval shelters for herd-boys remain in the south part of the island. The farmhouses were scattered through and north of the present village area, with an outlying settlement just

Rocks at village

East coast from south

Spouting Cave

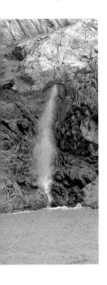

north of Columba's Bay where there are traces of house-ruins, cultivation-ridges and stock-enclosures.

The present agricultural landscape of dispersed croft-houses, standing in their own rectilinear enclosures and with access to the common grazings, was created by the Argyll estate soon after 1800, along with the village street (p. 9) for landless cottagers. Older methods of cultivation remained in use, and some of the short narrow 'lazy-bed' ridges dug with the spade or *caschrom* ('foot-plough'), visible north of Dùn Cùl Bhuirg and in many other areas, may belong to the period of population-pressure before the potato famines of the 1840s. Following that crisis, which brought heavy emigration, several crofts were amalgamated into larger farms and extensive drainage of the rough grazings allowed a great increase in the stock of sheep. At the present day there are two farms and eighteen crofts, organised in two townships. Many of the thatched houses were rebuilt with slated roofs in the late 19th century, although some thatch survived in the village until the 1930s.

At present Iona has a permanent population of almost one hundred, and several families retain their Gaelic language and oral traditions. Crofting and fishing remain important in the island's economy, along with boat-hiring and other services for the hundreds of thousands of visitors who come each year. The school, whose history extends back to the 1770s, occupies a Victorian building, and both hotels originated in the same period, while newer facilities include several shops, a community hall and a surgery, and a vehicle ferry for the use of permanent residents.

Sandy bay at village

(below right) Sea-pinks

Printed in the UK for HMSO by (13218) Dd293065 C150 2/95